Mythical Realms of THE NORSE UNIVERSE

TITLES IN THIS SERIES INCLUDE:

Creatures of Norse Mythology
Epic Quests and Adventures of Norse Mythology
Gods and Goddesses of Norse Mythology
Heroes and Villains of Norse Mythology
Mythical Realms of the Norse Universe

Discovering Norse Mythology

Mythical Realms of THE NORSE UNIVERSE

Don Nardo

San Diego, CA

Printed in the United States

For more information, contact:
ReferencePoint Press, Inc.
PO Box 27779
San Diego, CA 92198
www.ReferencePointPress.com

LIBRARY OF CONGRESS CATALOGING-IN-PUBLICATION DATA

Names: Nardo, Don, 1947- author.
Title: Mythical realms of the Norse universe / by Don Nardo.
Description: San Diego, CA : ReferencePoint Press, Inc., 2026. | Series: Discovering Norse mythology | Includes bibliographical references and index.
Identifiers: LCCN 2024049076 | ISBN 9781678210366 (library binding) | ISBN 9781678210373 (ebook)
Subjects: LCSH: Mythology, Norse--Juvenile literature. | Cosmology, Norse--Juvenile literature.
Classification: LCC BL860 .N268 2026 | DDC 398.20948--dc23/eng/20241206
LC record available at https://lccn.loc.gov/2024049076

CONTENTS

A World Filled with Wonder

The incredibly handsome god twisted and turned on his bed, wracked by a series of terrible dreams. He saw weird, monstrous shapes darting around, sometimes coming uncomfortably near and seemingly threatening to snuff out his life. Suddenly he awoke in a clammy sweat. What were those hostile, frightening creatures that had disturbed his rest?, he wondered.

Jumping out of bed, Baldur, the Norse deity of light and purity, wasted no time in recounting his lurid nightmare to several fellow gods. One of those divine beings, their leader, Odin—often called the All-Father—was particularly disturbed by what he heard. This was partly because he was Baldur's father, and a good father naturally worries about his children's well-being. Odin was also concerned because, as a powerful magician himself, he knew that dreams often foreshadowed future events. And there was a chance that someone or something might be planning to harm Baldur.

Baldur
The Norse god of light and purity

At that moment Odin remembered that he knew of a seeress—a witch who could foretell the future. She inhabited a hidden grave in Niflheim, the gloomy underworld. Odin offered to consult with her to try to unravel the meaning of Baldur's disquieting dreams.

To that end, the All-Father mounted his eight-legged horse, Sleipnir, and descended into Niflheim's damp, swirling mists. Reaching the witch's ancient gravesite, he chanted some mystical spells to summon her spirit. According to mythologist Kevin Crossley-Holland, the ghost asked, "Who is this stranger who forced me up?" The god identified himself, after which the seeress warned that Baldur was doomed to be murdered. Distressed at those words, Odin asked, "Who will slay Baldur and drain the life-blood of Odin's son?"[1]

The pale specter shuddered at that question and refused to answer. But she did tell the All-Father that Baldur's tragic end would be the first in a series of events that would lead to the death of all the gods. After uttering those words, the eerie apparition sank back down into the ground. Seconds later, with a heavy heart, Odin mounted his faithful steed and galloped upward toward the world's surface.

Living at the Center of the World

The story of how Baldur's dream foreshadowed his later demise was one of the most often told and retold myths of the Norse, also frequently called the Vikings. Robust, resilient, and often warlike, they inhabited large sections of Denmark and Scandinavia in Europe's early to mid-medieval period. Between about 800 and 1000 CE, bands of Vikings often raided the coasts of the British Isles, France, and other parts of western Europe.

The Norse conception of the universe and their place within it was unique among the worldviews of other ancient peoples. "The Vikings thought that the world they lived in on a day-to-day basis was just a tiny sliver of a vast and richly varied universe," says Daniel McCoy, a noted scholar of Norse culture. "That enormous world," he goes on, "was invisible to the average eye."[2] The belief was that all the mountains, meadows, towns, lakes, and other aspects of the lands where they and other peoples dwelled constituted a small portion of a gigantic tree. The main branches and roots of that so-called World Tree were so far away, the Vikings held, that no humans could see them.

World Tree
In Norse mythology, the physical structure of the universe

Origins of Norse Mythology

Two major beliefs rested at the core of this unusual view of the universe. The first was that the human-inhabited lands made up a realm—a sort of large continent—located in the great tree's center. They called that central landmass Midgard, meaning "Middle Earth." According to this view, Midgard was surrounded by a circular ocean so wide that people could never cross it. And the World Tree's many other realms were situated on the far side of that vast sea. This concept of existence seems fanciful today. Yet it made sense to the Norse because it fit the physical reality that they observed. No matter how far people traveled on land, in any direction, they eventually encountered the shores of a seemingly boundless ocean.

An Enchanted Universe

The second core belief that shaped the Norse view of the universe was a powerful magical element, or quality, that pervaded all things. The myth in which Odin traveled to the underworld and conjured up the ghost of a dead witch was only one of many tales that described a seemingly enchanted universe. It was thought to be permeated by countless mystical beings and forces, some visible and others invisible. And all the events of people's lives were supposedly influenced by fate, the will of various gods, or in McCoy's words, "by lesser numinous [supernatural] beings such as land spirits, elves, dwarves and giants. Any field, mountain, moor, forest, sea, stone, house, hall, person, custom, or event could potentially hold and transmit an intimation of some kind of divine presence. Magic was a seamless part of life."[3]

This view of a world infused with mystical qualities was not a fantasy invented by one Viking poet or another. Rather, the collection of Norse myths that remain so popular and entertaining today imprinted itself on early Viking society. These tales then passed orally from one generation to another, showing people of all walks of life their supposed place in a world filled with wonder, spirituality, and unknowable mysteries.

The Era of Creation

A very, very long time ago, there was no ground to stand on. Nor was there a sky above, with a sun, moon, and stars shining. What is more, below that vast vault of blackness, no seas, mountains, or forests yet existed. "That was the age when nothing was," a surviving medieval European document states. "There was no sand, nor sea, nor cool waves, no earth, nor sky, nor grass there. Only Ginnungagap."[4] In the language spoken by the early Norse inhabitants of Scandinavia, the word *ginnung* meant "filled with magic." And a "gap" was, as it still means in English today, a void. So Ginnungagap was a gigantic hollow space, empty except for some invisible, mysterious magical properties swirling around within it.

There were no people yet to witness all that nothingness and darkness. Therefore, no one was around to keep track of time, so no one will ever know how long ago Ginnungagap existed. It may have been a hundred or even a thousand centuries ago.

More certain, according to the Norse creation myths, at some unknown point in time Ginnungagap became surrounded by very different physical elements. On one side was a monstrous mass of intense fire called Muspelheim. And on the other side there formed a wide expanse of solid ice—Niflheim. Now and then bright flares of flame from Muspelheim leaped across Ginnungagap, landed in Niflheim, and melted some of its ice.

As time progressed, those tiny water droplets clung together into a big liquid blob that revolved around Ginnungagap. As that moist mass passed by blazing Muspelheim, it grew hotter, and that warmth somehow combined with the magical proper-

Ginnungagap
The huge area of nothingness that existed before the world's creation

ties on the edges of Ginnungagap. As a result, there eventually emerged a living being, a huge primordial creature known as Ymir.

At first, as Ymir continued to revolve around the great void, he did nothing but sleep. How long he dozed within his warm cocoon of supernaturally infused water no one can say. Finally, lumps formed inside his left armpit. These grew into smaller versions of himself and became what the Norse called giants. Soon afterward, a six-headed giant emerged from the calf of Ymir's right leg. These were the forefathers of the members of the race of giants that inhabited the strange, fascinating world described in the world-famous Norse myths.

Purposes of the Creation Myths

Today the story of Ymir's birth, the other Norse creation tales, and the myths of the Norse gods and heroes are told and retold mainly for their entertainment value. For example, each time a new installment of the Marvel Comics series of movies about Thor, Loki, and the other Norse gods appears, millions of eager fans rush to theaters in countries around the world. Back in the Viking age, by contrast, those myths served very different purposes. First, they informed the residents of the Norse lands about who the gods were, the parts of nature they controlled, and what they expected of humans.

Second, several of the Norse myths, in particular the creation stories, explained why nature works the way it does. By hearing such tales repeatedly recited beginning as young children, says Kevin Crossley-Holland, people learned "why the sun appears in the morning and disappears at night." They also acquired an explanation for how the moon moves across the sky at night. In both cases, the Norse envisioned divine beings carrying those celestial bodies across the heavens in magnificent, magical chariots. In addition, says Crossley-Holland, the creation tales told "why the wind blows, why it thunders . . . [and] why each animal has different characteristics."[5]

This photo shows a poster for the movie, Thor: Ragnarok. *Norse creation myths have been retold many times, including in the popular Marvel movies.*

Furthermore, and no less importantly, the Norse creation stories provided people with an explanation of how the universe itself came to be. They told how the gods emerged and how those deities made human beings. In the often cited words of the late, noted French anthropologist Mircea Eliade, "To know the myths is to learn the secret of the origin of things."[6] Experts refer to such origin stories as etiological myths.

Dim-Witted Giants and an Ice-Licking Cow

The etiological myths of the Norse begin with the great void, Ginnungagap, and how the first living being, Ymir, formed within a magical bubble of water spinning around it. A dull, nearly mindless creature, Ymir had the singular capacity to reproduce asexually; that is, he did not require a mate. That is why smaller giants, both male and female, regularly arose from his armpit.

Meanwhile, the magically infused water still dripping away from Niflheim's icy ground congealed into another creature, this one an immense cow. Ymir, who was glad to have its milk for nourishment, named it Audhumla. The big bovine being itself needed nourishment, and to obtain it she licked at a mound of salty ice at Niflheim's edge. Soon, quite unexpectedly, wrote the late British mythologist Brian Branston, as she licked the ice "something new began to appear. By evening of the first day her questing tongue had licked out the hair of a man. All the next day she nuzzled and slobbered until a man's head appeared. By the third day she had licked a complete man into shape."[7]

This new individual, Buri by name, was unlike all the earlier living things that had emerged. He possessed intelligence, considerable longevity, and most important of all, various supernatural powers. Surveying the situation, Buri concluded that he did not want to spend untold eons in the company of dim-witted giants and an ice-licking cow. He longed to be among rational, congenial beings like himself. So he decided to become the forerunner of a race of gods. To that end, he mated with one of the female giants that had sprung from Ymir and with her produced a son named Bor. In his turn, Bor sired three sons of his own, whom he named Odin, Vili, and Ve.

A Tremendous Cosmic Building Project

Of the three new gods, Odin was without question the shrewdest and, with many magical qualities coursing through his body, the most powerful. He looked to the future and correctly came to two major conclusions. First, those in his family line and other beings like them had a chance to maintain control over and rule all that existed. This was possible, he reasoned, because they were both intelligent and powerful enough to do so. This may well have been the moment that he named his divine race the Aesir (a term derived from an Indo-European word, meaning "the breath of life").

Aesir
The race of Norse gods who dwelled in the realm of Asgard

Odin's second significant realization was that what then existed—consisting of some stretches of fire, ice, and nothingness—was not worth ruling. There needed to be an extensive, fully functioning universe, or world, for the Aesir in their potential glory to oversee. So he discussed the matter with his brothers, Vili and Ve, and they agreed that the best way forward was to construct a suitable world.

The three Aesir also agreed that they could get most of the materials they needed by slaying the otherwise useless Ymir and disassembling his gigantic body. Wasting no time, Odin and the others slit the giant's throat. Noted author and mythologist Neil Gaiman describes how every part the monstrous corpse was utilized in the tremendous cosmic building project that ensued:

> Odin and his brothers made the soil from Ymir's flesh. Ymir's bones they piled up into mountains and cliffs. Our rocks and pebbles, the sand and gravel you see [were] Ymir's teeth, and the fragments of bones that were broken and crushed by Odin and Vili and Ve in their battle with Ymir. The seas that girdle the world, these were Ymir's blood and his sweat. Look up into the sky: you are looking at the inside of Ymir's skull.[8]

This picture shows the giant, Ymir; the cow, Audhumla; and Buri, the humanlike creature that Audhumla had licked from the ice in a Norse creation myth.

How Do We Know About Yggdrasil?

Much of what is known today about Yggdrasil, the World Tree, comes from *Gylfaginning*, the opening section of the important thirteenth-century Norse document the *Prose Edda*. That section takes the form of a dialogue in which a legendary Swedish king, Gylfi, asks questions of three rulers who sit on their thrones. Gylfi asks about Yggdrasil, and part of their answer, excerpted here, describes some of the colorful creatures that share the great tree with the gods, humans, and giants:

> The ash [known as Yggdrasil] is the greatest and best of all trees. Its limbs stretch over the entire world and rise above heaven. Three roots of the tree hold it up and stretch out widely. One is among the Aesir, the second among the giants, where Ginnungagap used to be, the third stands over Niflheim. . . . A certain eagle sits in the limbs of the ash, and it knows a great deal, and between its eyes sits that hawk who is called Vedrfolnir. That squirrel which is called Ratatosk runs up and down the ash and carries malicious words between the eagle and [the dragon] Nidhogg.

Quoted in John Lindow, *Handbook of Norse Mythology*. Oxford, UK: ABC-CLIO, 2001, pp. 320–21.

The vast new world the early Aesir fashioned partly from Ymir's body and partly from sections of blazing Muspelheim and icy Niflheim was neither spherical nor square. Nor did it have any other simple-looking shape. Instead, it took the complex form of an unbelievably enormous ash tree. The Norse called it Yggdrasil, the World Tree. Within its massive branches, trunk, and roots were lodged numerous separate realms, or kingdoms, including one called Asgard, where the Aesir chose to dwell.

The First Humans

As it turned out, constructing the World Tree was only part of a succession of creative acts that Odin and his kin carried out. To produce more members of the growing Aesir family, for example, the All-Father married Frigg, the goddess of marriage and daughter of an earth spirit named Fjorgvin. That union produced a number of sons and daughters who took up residence in Asgard.

While that realm's divinities were multiplying, they learned of the existence of a second group of gods who called themselves the Vanir. Knowing that neither he nor any of the other Aesir had sired that rival divine family, Odin consulted Mimir, a deity known for his great wisdom. Mimir said that the origin of the Vanir was unknown, but there was a rumor they had appeared miraculously in the midst of the picturesque realm later named for them, Vanaheim. They were mainly overseers of agriculture and fertility, Mimir explained, and did not seem to possess powers as potent as those of the Aesir.

Deciding that the Vanir posed no threat to the gods of Asgard, Odin continued his ongoing work of creation. One day he and Vili and Ve were walking along a stretch of beach and noticed two large pieces of driftwood lying in the sand. One was ash wood, the other, elm wood. Powerful tides had tossed and dragged these objects around, imparting to them shapes that looked somewhat like torsos with arms and legs. And that gave the three gods an idea. What if there was a race of beings, they wondered, who physically looked like the gods but who lacked divine powers and would give the Aesir regular worship? With that in mind, Odin knelt beside one of the objects and breathed a spark of his divine spirit into it. He and his brothers then watched as the artifact began to move. In the minutes that followed, it transformed into a living woman, to whom the deities gave the name Elm.

After that, Odin knelt beside the second object. "Once more," Branston wrote, "he breathed on the thin bark and this time the figure of a man appeared in the wood." The three gods dubbed him Ash. "The two new beings, the first man and the first woman, looked at each other in full understanding, rose to their feet and embraced."[9] These first two human beings soon began having children, and the gods granted their race a homeland of their own in the World Tree—a realm called Midgard.

Creation Threatened by Conflict

As the stages of creation that the early members of the Aesir had set in motion continued, Odin noted that other races of beings

Heimdall was responsible for ensuring that only divine beings crossed Bifrost. He is pictured here guarding Bifrost.

existed besides gods and humans. There were also smaller creatures, among them the dwarfs and elves. They had developed from the numerous squirming maggots that had initially lived on Ymir's skin. Odin made sure that both dwarfs and elves had their own places to live among the World Tree's huge branches.

During this same period, the Aesir also created Bifrost, a magnificent, glittering, and quite permanent rainbow. Hundreds of miles in extent, it arched across the sky, forming a bridge that connected Asgard to Midgard. Odin wanted to make it easy for the gods to cross into the latter realm to keep track of the humans he and his brothers had recently created. By contrast, he did not want those mortals to have easy

Bifrost
A massive rainbow bridge that connected the realms of Asgard and Midgard

access to Asgard, so he assigned Heimdall, god of the constructive uses of fire, to guard Bifrost and allow only divine beings to cross it.

At some point not long after Bifrost's creation, an unexpected event occurred that temporarily halted the Aesir's grand process of creation. To Odin's surprise and dismay, he learned that the Vanir were not as harmless as he had first assumed. Over time, trust between the two groups eroded, and finally a full-scale war erupted.

During the conflict, the Vanir invaded Asgard, a bold move for which the Aesir were unprepared. Before Odin and his brethren could mount a counterattack, the Vanir unleashed magical spells that toppled many of their opponents' palatial homes. Eventually, the Aesir retaliated and attacked Vanaheim. Because the two groups appeared to be evenly matched, their members came to worry that the conflict might go on and on and destroy all the wonders the Aesir had recently created. So the opposing parties signed a peace treaty. Thereafter, parts of the two divine races merged. As a result, the Aesir acquired some new members, including Freya, goddess of beauty and love, and her brother, the fertility deity Frey.

Fortifying Asgard

All the gods came to regret the conflict. But on the positive side, it had taught the Aesir a valuable lesson; namely, that Asgard had no fortifications capable of keeping an invader out. The Vanir were no longer a threat; however, during the centuries of the era of creation, the giants who had earlier been spawned by Ymir had multiplied. Thousands of them now lived within the World Tree, and a majority of them hated Odin and the other gods. Clearly, Odin told Heimdall one day (in Gaiman's account), "We need a wall."[10]

About a week later a big, strong man dressed as a blacksmith asked for an audience with Odin. When the stranger stood before the All-Father, he said, "They say you need a wall built. I can build you a wall. Build it so high that the tallest giant could not climb it.

Loki's Ruse Backfires on Him

When Asgard's defensive wall was nearly finished, the trickster god Loki concocted a ruse to distract the builder long enough to let the deadline for completion pass. One of Loki's skills was shape-shifting, which allowed him to transform into the shape of any person or animal. This time he took the form of a mare, or female horse. As noted scholar of Norse culture William R. Short tells it, when the builder's stallion, Svadilfari, caught sight of the mare, he went "wild with desire. He tore apart his harness and chased after the mare. The mare ran into woods with the stallion close behind, and the builder chased after the two of them, trying to catch the stallion. All night long, the three tore through the woods. The next day, not much work was completed."

After Thor killed the builder, the gods ended up finishing the wall themselves. Meanwhile, Loki's scheme had unexpectedly backfired on him. When Svadilfari caught up with the "Loki-mare," the stallion had impregnated "her." And after a few months, the divine trickster gave birth to an eight-legged male foal. The embarrassed Loki gave it to Odin, who named it Sleipnir and cherished it ever after.

William R. Short, "The Wall of Ásgarð," Hurstwic. www.hurstwic.com.

. . . I can build it so well, by placing stone upon stone, that not an ant could find space enough to crawl through it. I will build you a wall that will last for a thousand [times a] thousand years."[11]

When Odin asked how long the job would take, the stranger first said three years, but after some haggling he agreed to do it faster. With the aid of his trusty horse Svadilfari, the man said, he would manage to complete the wall in just one year. Then the All-Father wanted to know how much the project would cost, and the stranger said that as payment he desired to marry the goddess Freya. The gods saw that price as far too steep. But they agreed to the deal anyway. They figured the stranger could not complete such an enormous task in only a year. And when he inevitably failed to finish in the time agreed upon, they could just send him away, unpaid, and finish the wall themselves.

This scheme turned out to be a mistake. In the morning of the last day of the allotted year, to the gods' astonishment the wall was nearly complete. Worried that the stranger would finish on time, Odin turned to Loki, god of lying and deceit. A master of mischief, Loki lured away the builder's horse, Svadilfari, and as a result the deadline was not met. The builder realized he had been cheated, flew into a rage, and threatened the lives of several gods. That prompted Odin's son Thor, god of thunder and lightning, to crush the man's skull with his magic hammer.

The gods then finished the wall themselves. With proper protection for Asgard in place, Odin and the other Aesir felt that the long process of world building that had begun with Ymir's death was at last complete. At that moment a new era began, one sometimes called Asgard's, and the world's, golden age. Lasting for untold centuries, it would be, in Branston's words, a time without war or strife when the gods would be "able to sleep untroubled with dreams or worries of any kind."[12]

CHAPTER TWO

Realms of the Living

The mighty Thor, god of thunder and lightning and chief protector of the Norse deities, leisurely made his way through a stretch of well-forested wilderness. He was somewhat unsure of whether he was still in Jotunheim, the main stronghold of the giants who dwelled in Yggdrasil, the vast World Tree. Perhaps, he thought to himself, he had already crossed into Midgard, the land inhabited by human beings.

Soon, the burly, red-bearded Thor, whose hammer was the most destructive weapon in existence, reached the shore of a riverlike inlet of the sea. Standing beside a small boat on the opposite bank was an elderly looking man wearing ragged peasant's clothes. Assuming the individual to be the ferryman, the thunder god called out to him and requested to cross the inlet. But the ferryman refused. As told in the medieval document now called the *Poetic Edda*, in a haughty tone of voice he said that the boat's owner "told me not to ferry highwaymen [robbers] or horse thieves, but good men alone."[13]

The quick-tempered Thor was taken aback by this unprovoked attack on his character. Figuring that identifying himself would intimidate the ferryman, he called out, "I am Odin's son!" When the ferryman remained silent, the god added, "With Thor you converse here!" Still, the ragged man stayed silent. Becoming increasingly exasperated, Thor demanded to know the man's name. The ferryman answered, "I am called Harbard."[14]

This was a lie. Although Thor did not realize it at the time, the ferryman was actually his father, Odin, leader of the divine Aesir. Well disguised, the elder deity began hurling one insult after another at his unsuspecting son, who grew angrier by the minute. In retaliation, Thor started bragging about his many feats of bravery and renown. He had slain many giants, he said, and all sorts of evil beings as well.

To this, the veiled Odin replied that Thor was a gutless coward who "dared in your terror neither to sneeze nor fart." Furious that someone had dared to insult him in such a manner, Thor bellowed, "Harbard, you pervert! I would knock you into hell if I could stretch over the water!" Moreover, "Your glibness with words will bring evil upon you if I decide to wade over the sound. Louder than the wolf I think you'll howl if you get a blow from my hammer!"[15]

The heated exchange continued for the rest of the afternoon. Finally, Thor realized that the ferryman was not going to take him across the inlet and stormed away, intent on finding another route across Midgard. It was several weeks later that Odin revealed the joke he had played. In a real fight, he admitted, his hammer-wielding son would surely win. But in a battle of wits, the All-Father would always prevail. With this, the embarrassed and somewhat slow-witted Thor had no choice but to agree.

A Largely Carefree Existence

Compared to the serious tone of a majority of the surviving Norse myths, the one in which Thor and his father, disguised as a ferryman, trade barbs contains humor and a certain charming quality. As historian Irina-Maria Manea points out, the tale consists of a verbal duel, in Norse terms, "a so-called *mannjafnadr*, a comparison of men, both [boasting] their superiority. The poem differs in tone from the others in the *Poetic Edda;* with its colloquial nature, [the story] seems more like a farce than anything to be taken seriously."[16]

That fact, combined with the setting of the story, is revealing. As it begins, Thor is enjoying a leisurely journey on his way home from an adventure. It may have occurred in the land of the giants, Jotunheim, since several Norse myths depict him battling giants (Jotnar). And Odin seems to have nothing better to do than play

The World Tree and its various realms, rivers, mountain ranges, and other geographical features contained the diverse inhabitants overseen by Odin and his fellow deities.

a silly, at times cruel, joke on his most famous son. The *Poetic Edda* does not place the story in any particular time frame. But it appears to be an era in which the gods enjoyed a largely jovial, carefree existence.

In fact, just such a time period is described in the annals of the Norse myths. It is the long era directly following the creation of the World Tree and its various realms, rivers, mountain ranges, and other geographical features. Modern mythologists often call it the golden age of Asgard (or of the Norse gods). During the period's seemingly countless centuries, the diverse inhabitants

A Goddess Comes to Midgard

One of the many Norse myths set in the human realm of Midgard featured a Swedish king named Gylfi. In this myth, a goddess named Gefjon—disguised as a beautiful, mortal woman—visited the king. She gained his trust by wining, dining, and complimenting him. The king liked her so much that he told her she could have as much of his land as she could plow in one day. The catch was that she could only do this with the help of four oxen. But instead of using ordinary oxen, Gefjon used four giant oxen. Coupled with her divine powers, she plowed many square miles of Gylfi's land. Then she broke that huge landmass away from Sweden and dragged it southward, mile after mile, causing numerous minor earthquakes in the process. Finally, she deposited that piece of land in the nearby country of Denmark, which happened to be her favorite human kingdom.

of the universal tree overseen by Odin and his fellow deities were largely at peace. It is true that now and then one of the Jotnar got up enough nerve to challenge one or another of Asgard's divine residents. But such episodes were few, trivial, and no serious threat to the Aesir's mastery of the world they had constructed.

From Asgard to Midgard

To help maintain that mastery, from time to time Odin went to the roof of his personal palace, Valaskjalf. And from there he climbed the tall, winding staircase leading to Hlidskjalf, the "High Seat," his special throne. Thanks to magical powers that he alone possessed, from that vantage he could both see and hear what was happening in the numerous realms located within Yggdrasil's immense, majestical framework.

Hlidskjalf
The special throne that allowed Odin to see into all the world's realms

From Odin's point of view, the world's closest regions were the many subdivisions of Asgard itself, the realm that occupied the highest point within the great tree. Valaskjalf was one of the mansions, or great halls, the All-Father maintained in his own territory. Featuring ceilings made of pure silver, the *Poetic Edda* states, Odin designed Valaskjalf "for himself in bygone days."[17]

Meanwhile, other members of the Aesir had their own sub-realms and palaces within Asgard. Baldur, the most popular god in the eyes of most of the World Tree's assorted residents, resided in a place called Breidablik. Thor and his wife, the fertility goddess Sif, dwelled in the mini kingdom of Thrudheim in a hall said to have 540 rooms. And Heimdall, who guarded Bifrost, the rainbow bridge, occupied an enormous citadel known as Himinbiorg. There, the *Poetic Edda* tells us, that stalwart deity "rules over his sanctuaries [and] the gods' glad watchman drinks good mead [a liquor made from honey] in the peaceful hall."[18]

Thor is pictured fighting the giants. He often went to Jotunheim, sometimes for a friendly visit, but often to right a wrong or settle a score.

Somewhat lower in Yggdrasil, and connected to Asgard via the arching rainbow bridge, loomed Midgard. The Norse frequently called this vast human-populated realm the *real world*. It consisted of all the places they could see and travel to, including Scandinavia, other parts of Europe, western Asia, and northern Africa.

Many Norse myths had Midgard as their central setting. Considering that people were its chief residents, it is not surprising that most of those stories involved human rulers and heroes. Of the heroic myths based in Midgard, one of the most famous involved a valiant warrior who came to be called Sigurd the Dragonslayer. The dragon in question had originally been a human male named Fafnir. The gods had given Fafnir's father a hoard of jewels, and Fafnir killed the older man, stole the treasure, turned himself into a dragon, and escaped into the wilderness. Fafnir's brother, Regin, asked the renowned fighter Sigurd to intervene. And employing the equally famous, powerful sword Gram, the hero slew the beast and recovered the treasure.

Forays into Giant-Land

Bordering Midgard, and to a lesser extent Asgard, was Jotunheim, the immense region allotted to the many giants who dwelled in the World Tree. Much of "Giant-Land," as it was often informally called, consisted of wide, rock-filled plains, deep forests with towering trees, and mountain ranges covered with permanent layers of ice. The giants called their capital Utgard, which meant "beyond the fence." Utgard was a huge and formidable walled town, but it was not the only such fortress in Jotunheim. This realm featured numerous other fortresses and castles. One of the most important was Thrymheim, home of the powerful, mean-spirited giant Thrym.

Jotunheim figured prominently in the Norse myths in part because of the ongoing rivalry and mutual dislike between the giants and the Aesir. Individual giants sometimes invaded the gods' realm. Typically, those transgressors crossed over the Ifingr, the deep river that separated Jotunheim from one corner of Asgard. Before they

Proof of the Legendary Giants?

The idea that giants, called Jotnar by the Vikings, existed in Jotunheim, as well as some other realms within the World Tree, developed early among the Norse. This concept may have been based on the same reasoning employed by some late medieval writers, including the thirteenth-century Danish historian Saxo Grammaticus. He offered so-called proof for the existence of the legendary giants by suggesting that the many large ancient stone monuments found across northern Europe could only have been built by such creatures. He said in part:

> The fact that the land of Denmark was once inhabited by a race of giants is attested by the huge boulders found next to ancient burial mounds and caves. If anyone doubts whether or not this was carried out by superhuman power, let him ponder the heights of certain mounds and then say, if he can, who carried such huge rocks to their tops. Anyone considering this wonder must reckon it unthinkable that ordinary human strength could lift such bulk to that height.

Quoted in Andy Orchard, *Dictionary of Norse Myth and Legend*. London: Cassell, 1997, p. 55.

could do any serious damage to the deities' palaces, however, one of those divine beings—most often Thor—neutralized the threat.

Conversely, Thor frequently entered Jotunheim for one reason or another. On occasion he went to visit one of the few giants on friendly terms with the gods. But more often he went to Giant-Land to right a wrong or settle a score. After Thrym stole Thor's hammer, for instance, Thor traveled to Thrymheim disguised as Freya, goddess of beauty, recovered the weapon, and promptly used it to slaughter Thrym and several dozen other giants.

For the Norse, such tales about divine retribution against the giants were not only entertaining but also filled with deeper meaning about the nature of life and the cosmos. In a very real sense, the gods stood for civilization, order, and justice, whereas the giants represented barbarism, chaos, and injustice. In Viking eyes, therefore, Thor's forays into Jotunheim were necessary to maintain the natural order of things. "When Thor smote the giants with the hammer," scholar Daniel McCoy writes, "he was defending the cosmos and banishing the forces of chaos."[19]

More Diverse Realms

While Jotunheim is described often in the surviving Norse myths, another of the diverse realms composing the World Tree is rarely mentioned and remains mysterious. That shadowy domain was Vanaheim. The stronghold of the Vanir, the deities who fought the Aesir during the era of creation, Vanaheim was said to be situated on the opposite side of Asgard from Giant-Land. The Norse usually pictured the Vanir's homeland much as they did Asgard—as containing lush landscapes filled with flowers and enjoying perfect weather conditions.

Not far from Vanaheim lay another physically attractive realm, Alfheim, homeland of the light elves. The latter, some rumors claimed, may have been related by blood to the Vanir, although no one who lived in the great tree knew for sure whether that was true. At some point, the fertility god Frey took charge of Alfheim. Although he was not himself an elf, he had originally been one of the Vanir and thereby possibly related to the elves. According to the *Poetic Edda*, "Alfheim the gods gave to Frey in bygone days as a tooth-payment."[20] (In Viking culture, children routinely offered their lost teeth to Odin. In return, he supposedly conferred good luck on them. And it may be that Frey was gifted the elf kingdom after losing some teeth.)

Alfheim
The realm of the light elves

Somewhere to the north of Vanaheim and Alfheim, lodged deep beneath ground level, was Nidavellir, the realm of the dwarfs. They were widely renowned for their expertise as craftspeople, including blacksmiths, goldsmiths, silversmiths, sword and spear makers, and so forth. McCoy describes their underground world—lit by torches and candlelight—as a highly intricate "subterranean complex of mines and forges."[21]

One thing all these realms had in common was that they supported populations of living beings. The same was true of two large regions that had been totally barren before the acts of creation set in motion by the Aesir. These were the great ice realm of Niflheim and the fiery expanse known as Muspelheim. Perhaps not surprisingly, for numerous centuries those inhospitable wastelands remained destitute of life. But eventually, as the population of Jotunheim expanded, some of the giants born there ventured away to less occupied lands. Those who settled in Niflheim became known as the ice giants, and the residents of Muspelheim acquired the name fire giants. Among the latter was Surt, who wielded a white-hot sword and, like so many of the giants, hated the Aesir.

Travelers Through the Realms

Thus, the realms of the living beings within the World Tree were numerous and often extremely large. Yet that did not deter some residents of one region from traveling to other areas. Thor's fairly frequent excursions to Jotunheim constituted only one of several examples.

No less renowned, nor less important, than Thor's journeys to Giant-Land were Heimdall's many trips to Midgard. Heimdall's chief duty was guarding Bifrost, the rainbow bridge connecting Asgard to Midgard. But he sometimes made it his business to intervene in situations in which he felt he could make the lives of gods or humans better in some way. From his lofty castle, Himinbiorg, he kept watch over the state of human civilization in Midgard and was initially disappointed at what he saw. As McCoy puts it, "At this time humankind was wayward. No one knew what his proper work should be, and no one knew who should command whom, and toward what ends. Heimdall set out to remedy this situation by organizing humankind into a true society, one with classes, ranks, and titles."[22]

To carry out this massive project, Heimdall made many trips to Midgard, a land thousands of miles in extent, and eventually he visited almost every village. Often, he sired children with local women. And in each case, when a child grew up he or she knew his or her proper social status. In this way, there developed a system featuring clear-cut social divisions, among them nobles, merchants, soldiers, and farmers.

Meanwhile Heimdall's father, Odin, became a frequent traveler too. The All-Father did not confine himself to the human realm, however. Instead, at one time or another he journeyed to every region of vast Yggdrasil and even visited some of the little known niches hidden in the great tree's tangled roots. Most often his motive was to search for new wisdom, since he was obsessed with acquiring as much knowledge as possible.

One of these trips took Odin to a little-known spot situated on the far side of Jotunheim. In a secret grotto containing a deep pool of dark water, he encountered Mimir, god of wisdom. The latter told the visitor he could drink from the pond and thereby obtain hidden knowledge, but only by giving up one of his eyes.

Even after sacrificing an eye, the leader of the Aesir felt there was much more to learn, so he traveled southward through several realms. This time his goal was to unravel secret knowledge, including how to heal the sick and how to see partway into the future. Such enigmas were said to exist within written symbols

One day Odin met Gunnlod, who was forced to guard vats of magical mead. The two fell in love and she later gave birth to a son named Bragi.

Mimir
The Norse god of wisdom

called runes. The search for those secrets took Odin down to Yggdrasil's lowest, darkest level, near one of the world's dismal domains of the dead.

Still another long journey through multiple realms gained the All-Father the gift of the Mead of Poetry, a drink that imparted the ability to express oneself in beautiful, moving language. The journey took him down into a murky cavern. There he found a female giant named Gunnlod, who was trapped there, having been forced to guard large vats of the magical mead. The two fell in love, and later she gave birth to a son named Bragi. Odin made him the god of poetry, who subsequently traveled throughout the World Tree, reciting inspiring stories and verses. In this way, mythologist Donna Jo Napoli writes, "poetry arose and endured, just as it does today no matter where you wander."[23] At least for a while, Yggdrasil's diverse realms of the living shared some cherished moments of peace and happiness.

Realms of the Dead

The legendary Danish king Hadingus, more often called Hadding, sat on the wide terrace that extended outward from his bedchamber. As he did most mornings before eating breakfast, he watched the morning sunlight dissolve the drifting mists that had collected in the valley below the night before. Suddenly, the ruler heard a noise from the chamber behind him. Surely, he thought, his servants knew better than to disturb him at that hour.

Hadding arose and entered the bedchamber, fully expecting to reprimand one of his maids. But to his surprise he found an unknown woman standing before him. Wearing an ankle-length cloak, she ignored his demand that she give her name. Smiling, she held out to him some odd-looking but fragrant herbs, which immediately captured his attention. He asked her where she had gotten them, and she offered to take him to that place.

A Strange Journey

As if in a trance, Hadding eagerly followed the mysterious woman out of the palace and through some woods until they reached a path that descended underground. For hours they strode downward, passing through valleys and forests and meadows, none of which seemed familiar to the king. Finally, they came to some fields where the strange herbs grew in abundance. The king noticed a basket lying nearby and proceeded to fill it with the aromatic plants.

Hadding expected to carry the basket back to his kingdom. But his female guide bade him follow her farther downward, and he obeyed. Soon, they reached a raging river filled with spears, swords, and other weapons. This was Gioll, the woman told him, the turbulent moat that encircled Helheim, the gloomy realm of the dead. Downstream, Hadding saw a bridge that crossed the river and a female giant standing on the opposite bank. That must be Modgud, the king told himself, guardian of the entrance to Helheim. Sure enough, as he and his guide drew close to the bridge, Hadding could see looming behind the giantess a towering wall with a huge gate. Hadding had heard that that foreboding portal, called Helgrindr, was guarded by a monstrous hound called Garm. The belief was that the beast tore apart anyone who was not destined to dwell forever in the realm of death.

Modgud
A female giant who guarded the bridge leading into Helheim

By this time Hadding was so afraid that he refused to go any farther. He watched as his companion walked across the bridge and pulled a live rooster from her cloak. Tearing the creature's head off, she flung the carcass toward the great wall. Seconds later, the rooster sprang back to life and crowed loudly. At that moment Hadding suddenly found himself back on his terrace. He wondered if it had all been a bizarre dream. Or had Odin, leader of the gods, given him this vision for some reason? The latter seemed more likely, in that Odin had earlier offered to advise the king on important matters of state. Even so, it was said that for the rest of his days Hadding never learned for sure which of those scenarios was true.

Life and the Afterlife Side by Side

The mythical Norse realm of Helheim, also called simply Hel, had a special place in the religious beliefs and associated myths of the Norse. Later Christians saw it as more or less the equivalent of the Christian hell. But this was decidedly not the case. Daniel McCoy explains that

> apart from the fact that Hel and Hell are both realms of the dead, located beneath the ground, the two concepts have nothing in common. . . . [To the Norse] where one goes after death isn't any kind of reward for moral behavior or pious belief, or punishment for immoral behavior. . . . The dead in Hel spend their time doing the same kinds of things that Viking Age men and women did: eating, drinking, fighting, sleeping, and so forth. It wasn't a place of eternal bliss or torment as much as it was simply a continuation of life somewhere else.[24]

Valhalla (illustrated) was a realm that hosted the souls of brave warriors who had died in battle.

Funeral for a Viking Ruler

Viking funerals could be elaborate affairs, especially for kings and other important military leaders whose spirits probably journeyed to Valhalla or one of the other death realms. One such funeral was described by tenth-century Muslim traveler Ibn Fadlan. The extravagant ceremony, which he witnessed in 922 on a Baltic Sea beach, was for a local king. Ibn Fadlan described the celebrants chopping up a dog, two horses, a cow, and some chickens and tossing the pieces onto a moored ship. Next, he saw them kill a female slave and lay her body near that of the king in the center of the ship. Finally, Ibn Fadlan recalled, "the deceased's next of kin approached and took hold of a piece of wood and set fire to it. He walked backwards . . . [and] ignited the wood that had been set up under the ship. . . . Then the [other] people came forward with sticks and firewood. Each one carried a [flaming] stick. . . . The wood caught fire, and then the ship . . . and all it contained [burned to ashes]."

Quoted in Mark Miller, "The 10th Century Chronicle of the Violent, Orgiastic Funeral of a Viking Chieftain," History, Archaeology, Folklore and So On, April 25, 2015. https://historyandsoon.wordpress.com.

Although Helheim featured prominently in many myths, it was just one of multiple death realms in the Vikings' belief system. More than any other factors, entrance to some of these other realms depended on how a person died. The realm known as Valhalla, for example, hosted the souls of brave warriors who had died in battle. And the realm called Ran was the final resting place for people who drowned at sea.

What was most important to the Vikings about the various death realms was how they fit into the overall, grand Norse vision of the cosmos. As they saw it, in addition to the various realms of the living, the World Tree supported multiple realms of the dead. Life and the afterlife therefore existed in a sense side by side in ways unique to Norse religious beliefs.

The Queen of the Dead

One key aspect of Helheim that made it stand out among the Norse death realms was that it was the final destination of the vast majority of people. One did not have to be a valiant warrior to enter Helheim. Rather, it was populated by the souls of ordinary people—farmers, laborers, merchants—and sometimes even by some of the gods. Its exact location was disputed. Some myths suggested that it was part of the large, frozen land of Niflheim. In those stories Niflheim doubled as the home of the ice giants and the greater underworld. Other tales claimed that Helheim was situated far below Yggdrasil's massive roots.

Loki's daughter, Hel, was the queen of Helheim and was generally viewed as the goddess of death. Hel dwelled in a large, eternally moist and moldy castle.

While its exact location was a topic for speculation, no one questioned who controlled it. When the World Tree was still young, Odin named Loki's daughter, Hel, queen of Helheim. As such, she was generally viewed as the goddess of death. According to some myths, half of her face was fair and beautiful and the other half rotten and ugly.

The surviving medieval document now known as the *Prose Edda* claims that Hel dwelled in a large, eternally moist and moldy castle called Eljudnir, along with assorted servants and slaves. Two of those helpers, Ganglati and Ganglot, were apparently slow moving, perhaps even lazy. Both names translate from the old Norse language as "lazy walker." It may be that Hel's assistants did not need to be agile or quick, since the souls they oversaw had no way of escaping. Once a spirit entered Helheim, it could not leave unless Hel herself released it.

Trying to Rescue Noble Baldur

That reality was emphasized starkly in Hel's best-known myth. That dramatic tale begins in Asgard, a sunlit space far removed from Hel's somber subterranean kingdom. One day several of the gods gathered in a meadow to play games, and Baldur, god of light and virtue, became the center of attention. This was hardly surprising. As mythologist Hamilton W. Mabie ably tells it, Baldur "was the most god-like of all the gods, because he was the purist and the best. Wherever he went his coming was like the coming of sunshine, and . . . when men's hearts were white like light, and their lives clear as the day, it was because Baldur was looking down on them with those soft, clear eyes."[25]

The games would take a very dark turn, however. Baldur's mother, Frigg, thought it would be fun to show how much all beings and objects in the universe loved her son. At her urging, all agreed that they would never harm him. With that promise in hand, the gods embarked on a game of tossing rocks and spears and other objects at Baldur. They then watched in delight as the rocks and spears and other objects bounced off him with no effect—in keeping with their promise to never harm the god of light and virtue.

The deceitful Loki, who had long been jealous of Baldur, decided he had had enough of this sport. Somehow, he found out that one object in the universe had not made the promise. That object was mistletoe. Taking advantage of that fact, Loki secretly attached some mistletoe to the point of a spear, which as a result was now potentially lethal. He gave the weapon to Baldur's brother, Hodur, god of winter and darkness. Hodur hurled the spear at Baldur, assuming that it would just bounce off like all the others. Instead, it killed the god of light almost instantly.

As the Aesir mourned their loss, Baldur's grief-stricken mother pointed out that her son's spirit now rested in Helheim. In desperation, she pleaded with the Aesir to at least attempt to recover Baldur's soul. Hermod, Odin's steadfast messenger, stepped forward. According to Neil Gaiman's account of the story, Hermod said, "I will go to Hel. I will bring back Baldur the beautiful."[26]

Hermod
Odin's faithful messenger

For days brave Hermod rode Odin's swift steed Sleipner across diverse realms, until he finally reached the dark caverns of Helheim. Standing before the queen of the dead, he demanded, in Odin's name, that Hel release Baldur's noble spirit. But she refused. Only if every being and object in the universe cried for Baldur, she said, would she let him go. In the days that followed, the resourceful Hermod, aided by other messengers chosen by Odin, hurried throughout the known world, urging everyone to weep for Baldur. All agreed, except for a single female giant named Thokk, which meant that Baldur's soul remained trapped forever in Helheim. (Not long afterward, the Aesir discovered that Thokk was really the wily Loki in disguise.)

Feasting in Odin's and Freya's Halls

One major regret that Odin subsequently voiced was that his beloved son had died by treachery rather than in battle. If Baldur had fallen as a warrior, the All-Father pointed out, he would have

A Pivotal Place on Valhalla's Menu

That the warriors who dwelled in Odin's magical hall Valhalla ate well is attested by a surviving myth revolving around a large boar named Saehrimnir. Each evening when the fighters entered the dining hall, the main fare was none other than Saehrimnir. Earlier in the day, Odin's official chef, Andhrimnir, slaughtered the unfortunate animal and roasted the pieces in a huge pot that was suspended above a fire in a massive hearth in Valhalla's kitchen. The Valkyries, who had previously carried the warriors from the battlefield, now served the meat to the heroes.

The strange occurrence of the same large boar being roasted and eaten every night was made possible by Odin's potent magic. When that deity first built Valhalla, he cast a special spell. It ensured that each night, after supper, Saehrimnir would spring back to life and his flesh swiftly grow back. As a result, the tasty creature was never able to escape from its pivotal place on Valhalla's evening menu.

been eligible to enter one of the two most coveted of the many death realms. The first, located within the boundaries of Asgard, was Valhalla. Overseen by Odin himself, it was the final destination of the leading *einherjar*, the courageous warriors who had died in battle.

The journey to Valhalla began mere seconds after such a fearless fighter fell, as told in the myth about the tenth-century Norwegian ruler Eric Bloodaxe. Flying back and forth above the battlefield, and invisible to the living soldiers, including King Eric, were swarms of Valkyries. They were supernatural female beings whose name means "choosers of the slain." Among them were Brunhilda (meaning "Bright Battle"), Sigrun ("Victory Ruse"), and Svava ("Sleep Maker"). Their primary task was to carry the slain heroes to Valhalla. When Eric fell dead, therefore, one of these warrior women, possibly Sigrun, rushed to him. Lifting up his soul, she bore it off toward Valhalla.

According to the medieval poem *Eiriksmal*, the famously wise Odin knew that Eric's spirit, along with those of some of his fellow fighters, would arrive soon. He told a fellow god that he had foreseen "before daybreak that I was preparing Valhalla for a slain army. I awakened the einherjar, asking them to get up to strew [spread out] the benches and to rinse the drinking cups. I asked the Valkyries to bring [extra] wine, as if a leader should come."[27]

When Eric's soul reached Valhalla, he was impressed to see that its massive walls were constructed from large spear shafts and the roof was covered by warriors' shields. Inside the hall itself were benches and tables for feasting and lounging. Meanwhile, above the front gate hung the skeleton of a monstrous wolf. Soon, Eric was happily feasting with Odin and the rest of the fighters who dwelled in the All-Father's hall.

Not all dead warriors ended up in Valhalla, however. That special place was reserved for the most noble and heroic of their ranks. The Valkyries transported the rest of the spirits of brave fighters to another section of Asgard. Called Folkvangr, meaning "Field of the People," it was supervised by the goddess Freya. Her mansion there, known as Sessrumnir, was big, stately, and covered by intricate wood carvings of animals.

The einherjar who entered Sessrumnir took their seats at the enormous dining table. Soon, they saw the goddess make an imposing entrance, driving an ornately decorated chariot drawn by two large cats. After she dismounted and walked to her throne at the head of the table, they beheld the splendid cloak she wore. Called Valhamr, it was made of thousands of falcon feathers. In mythologist Kevin Crossley-Holland's words, that magical garment "enabled her spirit to take the form of a bird, travel to the underworld, and come back with prophecies and knowledge of destinies."[28]

Other Destinations for Souls

In addition to Helheim, Valhalla, and Folkvangr, the Norse myths recognized other destinations for the souls of the dead. One, called Ran, was named for a sea goddess of that name. It was thought that she dwelled in a watery kingdom, called Ranarsalr, or "Ran's Hall," situated somewhere on the seafloor. Ruling with her, various myths say, was her husband, Aegir. A giant originally

The sea goddess Ran is pictured here beneath the water, with her husband Aegir standing above her. When sailors began to drown, Ran cast a special net over them and dragged them down to her domain.

from Jotunheim, he was said to possess certain magical powers, including the ability to breathe under water.

Supposedly, when sailors or other sea voyagers fell into the water and began to drown, Ran detected their plight. Hurrying to them, she cast a special net over them and dragged them down to her waterlogged domain. Also, if the ship in which the dead men had been traveling sank, she salvaged any valuables it held and added them to her ever-growing hoard of treasures.

Ran and her kingdom feature indirectly in a myth perpetuated by the Icelandic Norse. It appears in the *Saga of the People of Eyri*, a story about warring families in western Iceland in the 1200s. At one point, the leader of one of the families and several of his followers die when their ship capsizes near a rocky shore. The bodies are not found, and it is assumed that they ended up in Ran's net. Later, during the funeral ceremonies, the ghosts of the missing people briefly appear, their clothes soaked and dripping. The mourners are relieved to see this. They believe that Ran has sent them a sign that the souls of the drowned are safe in her embrace.

Still another death realm mentioned in a few Norse myths is Helgafjell, meaning "Holy Mountain." Several tales placed it in Iceland, although its exact location was never confirmed in the myths. It was said to be a quiet, peaceful place where the spirits of the dead resided in comfort. None of the myths explain why a few souls of ordinary folk went to Helgafjell while a far larger number ended up in the gloomier, less comfortable Helheim. Spoken of even less in the Norse myths is a sixth death realm, called Nastrond, meaning the "Corpse Shore." All that is known about it is that it was a small section of Helheim and that its residents suffered horrible tortures and other torments.

Nastrond
A small death realm in which the residents suffered terrible tortures

Thus, there was a considerable array of final destinations for the souls of the residents of the World Tree. Modern scholars find it regrettable that too often the surviving written sources offer scarce information about what those death realms were like and why a spirit went to one place rather than another.

What is more certain is that the people of the ancient Norse world believed in an afterlife and that they would eventually experience it. That belief—that there was continuity between the realms of life and realms of death—gave people a fair degree of comfort in their everyday lives. The late, great scholar of Norse civilization H.R.E. Davidson summed it up, saying that in general, death was "faced without undue fear. The emphasis in the myths is . . . on the importance not of holding onto life at any cost, but of acting in a way which will be long remembered when life is over. . . . A man's heroic deeds will win renown, and his fine qualities will be passed on to his descendants. Such is the noblest form of immortality, and the great gods themselves achieved no more."[29]

CHAPTER FOUR

Apocalypse and Aftermath

Baldur's dream, in which he saw a mysterious figure killing him, proved to be a pivotal moment in the grand saga portrayed in the Norse myths. Troubled by his son's description of that nightmare, Odin rode his trusty horse Sleipnir down into dimly lit Niflheim to consult with the ghost of a long-dead witch. As the All-Father knew well, the world he inhabited was filled with magical properties. That included the ability of various beings to predict future events. Odin put serious stock in such prophecies. So when the specter he visited told him that Baldur would indeed die and that his passing would herald the coming of the demise of the gods, Odin became worried and uneasy.

What made the leader of the Aesir particularly apprehensive was that the ghost's prediction lined up far too neatly with another disturbing prophecy he had heard hundreds of centuries before. Back when the World Tree was still new, the Norns had foretold of just such an ultimate doomsday. Those three aged sisters—Wyrd, Verdandi, and Skuld by name—dwelled in a cave lodged within the roots of the World Tree. Most humans, and most of the gods as well, were reluctant even to mention the three old hags. This was because the Norns were thought to know the eventual fate of the cosmos and all who lived within it. And nearly everyone was fearful to learn what that destiny might be.

Odin had never feared the weird sisters themselves. But he had long secretly dreaded that their ancient prophecy might actually become reality. Eventually, they had predicted, there

Norns
Three aged supernatural sisters who could foresee future events

would occur Ragnarok, the "Twilight of the Gods." In that tumultuous catastrophe, they said, the Aesir, along with human beings, would face an array of enemies. And in that final, furious battle, all involved would die and the universe would collapse into nothingness.

Odin hoped that the apocalypse—for he could not see it as anything other than that—would not come to pass. He even maintained a sliver of optimism, hoping that the Norns were somehow wrong. In his heart of hearts, however, the All-Father suspected that Ragnarok could not be avoided, and he began to prepare for the worst.

Seeing Fate as Pointless and Evil

Much like the mythological leader of the Aesir, the early medieval Vikings were convinced that the cataclysmic Ragnarok would eventually happen. The primary reason for that view was their belief in fate and the prophecies connected with it. Indeed, the myths, which played a central role in Norse religion, strongly emphasized the theme of destiny. It was thought that individual people had their personal destinies. And humanity and the world as a whole had a greater collective fate, which was to be destroyed, along with the gods, in a final, calamitous battle.

Just because the Vikings accepted this version of the future does not mean they liked it. In fact, they decidedly disliked what destiny seemed to have in store for their world. This was because it seemed to be so arbitrary and pointless. There was no specific reason, moral or otherwise, mentioned in the myths to explain why the Norns had made such a prophecy. It seemed to be based on nothing more than the whims of three cranky, though powerful, old women.

Furthermore, most Vikings did not like the idea that Ragnarok was said to be unavoidable. It seemed unfair to them that the destruction of the world described in the prophecy could not be stopped. As a result, fate itself was often looked on as mean-spirited and evil. "Indeed," says Daniel McCoy, "part of what made

The Norns and the World Tree are pictured. When the World Tree was still new, the Norns foretold of an ultimate doomsday.

fate 'evil' is that it would one day utterly destroy all of this beauty and meaning that was native to the god-crafted world."[30]

The myths surrounding Ragnarok affected Viking society in other ways. Namely, those stories helped shape Norse attitudes toward war, fighting, and what constituted honor, dishonor, and the concept of heroism. Viking warriors tended to be highly moved by how Odin, Thor, and the other Aesir reacted to the coming of Ragnarok. The gods, along with their human allies, refused to give up hope. In an awe-inspiring demonstration of courage and confidence, they were determined to resist to their last breath. As the late, great mythologist Edith Hamilton movingly phrased it, the Norse gods were aware

> that a day will come when they will be destroyed. Sometime they will meet their enemies and go down beneath them to defeat and death. Asgard will fall in ruins. . . . Nevertheless,

> the gods will fight for it to the end. Necessarily, the same is true of humanity. . . . They know that they cannot save themselves, not by any courage or endurance or great deed. Even so, they do not yield. . . . They will fight on the side of the gods and die with them.[31]

In Viking eyes, therefore, one could show contempt for fate by boldly resisting it. "There was no honor in merely passively surrendering to fate," McCoy writes. Rather, "honor was to be found in approaching one's fate as a battle to fight heroically, even if it was a battle one was ultimately doomed to lose."[32] This was perhaps the greatest lesson the Norse learned from their myths.

Initial Preparations for Doomsday

In those tales, Odin showed his own contempt for fate by deciding to resist the Norns' dire predictions of an end-of-times battle. Determined to fight to the death if necessary, he began making preparations for that awful conflict. First, he called on the einherjar, the souls of dead human soldiers living in Valhalla, to fight with him if Ragnarok did come. And to a man, they expressed their eagerness to follow the leader of the gods into that terrible fray.

So determined were the einherjar to give their all for the All-Father that many of them readied themselves to transform into berserkers. Known from real-life examples in Norse armies, these were warriors who became so psyched to fight that they entered a kind of wild frenzy. "The smell of blood and sour sweat seemed to intoxicate them," Brian Branston wrote, "doubling their physical strength and daring. Their nostrils flared, they pawed the ground, and their fingers on their axe handles and sword hilts sweated and itched to come to blows."[33]

Odin realized that gathering well-trained fighters would not be enough to defeat the enemies the gods and humans would face during Ragnarok. Those dark forces would include thousands of

Thor and the Midgard Serpent

From the Norns' prophecy, the gods knew that Loki's monstrous children would play major roles in the final battle, Ragnarok. That is why they tried to permanently bind the giant wolf Fenrir. The Aesir also wanted to neutralize Jormungander, also known as the Midgard Serpent and the World Serpent. In fact, at one point long before the approach of Ragnarok Thor came close to slaying the creature. He journeyed to Jotunheim, realm of the giants, and pretended to be an ordinary human. In that disguise, he persuaded a giant named Hymir to take him fishing in the waters lying between Jotunheim and Midgard. Thor suspected that Jormungander lurked somewhere in that waterway and planned to lure the monster out and kill it with his famous hammer. Using an ox's head as bait, the thunder god did come face-to-face with the serpent. But it managed to slither away into deep water. At that moment Thor did not realize that he and Jormungander were fated to meet again in a furious fight to the death during Ragnarok.

giants, most of whom hated the gods. So he told his son Thor to begin making periodic trips into Jotunheim and to kill any hostile giants he encountered.

Also formidable among the Aesir's enemies were all sorts of monstrous beings, including dragons, sea serpents, and zombies. Perhaps the most fearsome among them were three of Loki's children. He had sired them by mating with a sinister giantess named Angrbode, a name that meant "She Who Brings Grief." One of those awful offspring was Hel, the formidable queen of the abode of the dead. The other two were Fenrir, a giant, vicious wolf, and Jormungander, a huge, bloodthirsty, snakelike creature.

Angrbode

The female giant with whom Loki mated to produce three monstrous children

Binding the Great Wolf

Hoping to reduce the threat posed by Loki's frightful brood, Odin ordered the Aesir to track down and capture Fenrir. To that end, the war god Tyr led an expedition that succeeded in catching the great wolf and bringing it back to Asgard in a cage. The problem

This picture shows the Aesir capturing the wolf, Fenrir, as ordered by Odin.

was that the cage was not strong enough to hold the creature indefinitely. What was needed was a way to permanently bind Fenrir so that it could not take part in Ragnarok. For that purpose, Odin's blacksmiths forged several big iron chains. But the monster easily broke all those restraints.

Realizing that the Aesir lacked the means of keeping the giant wolf imprisoned, Odin turned to a group of dwarfs known for their expertise in metalwork. They accepted the challenge and soon delivered a fetter like none ever seen before. Called Gleipnir, it was so thin it was nearly invisible. Yet it was so strong that it kept Fenrir permanently captive. Other than the dwarfs who crafted it, no one—not even Odin—knew what components went into

Gleipnir
A nearly invisible, superstrong chain created by a group of dwarfs to bind the giant wolf Fenrir

making the shackle. When Odin asked about this, according to the *Prose Edda*, one of the dwarfs whispered, "the noise a cat makes in foot-fall, the beard of a woman, the roots of a rock, the sinews of a bear, the breath of a fish, and the spittle of a bird."[34]

Although the gods had scored an initial victory by binding the great wolf, they did pay a price for it. While using Gleipnir to secure Fenrir, Tyr strayed a bit too close to the beast's mouthful of sharp teeth. And in an instant the wolf bit off the god's right hand. Fortunately, Tyr took the loss in stride. It was a minimal price to pay, he told Odin, for removing a major threat to the existing world order.

The Pursuit of Loki

During the same period in which the Aesir were preparing for their prophesied climactic showdown with their enemies, they were also looking for Loki. Once the other gods learned that he had tricked Hodur into killing Baldur, the trickster had departed Asgard as fast as he could. He reasoned, correctly, that the other deities would vigorously pursue him and that if they caught him, they would severely punish him. So he fled to the summit of a remote mountain in a scarcely populated region of the World Tree.

The gods eventually found the divine fugitive, however. At the last moment he tried transforming himself into a fish and hiding in a pool of water. But he had morphed into animals so many times in the past that his pursuers suspected he had done so again. And when, still in fish form, he leaped from the pool in hopes of escaping, Thor caught him in a net.

The Aesir punished Loki by chaining him to some large rocks in a dark, damp cave. "To make his punishment the more terrible," Hamilton W. Mabie explains, "they hung a serpent over him." The creature relentlessly "dropped poison on his face,"[35] causing him excruciating pain.

The Slaughter During Ragnarok

As the forces of good and evil clashed in Ragnarok, the Norse gods met their end. But they did not die in vain. Each fought furiously, mustering every available ounce of strength and skill, and thereby took a terrible toll on the enemy ranks. At times a dying deity and the opponent expired together, as when the dependable Heimdall and the deceitful Loki slew each other. Similarly, Garm, the hateful hound who guarded the entrance to Helheim, fatally wounded the war god Tyr. But just as the latter breathed his last, he managed to dispatch the creature. Meanwhile, noble Odin battled the great wolf Fenrir. The beast roared and drooled and in a deft move swallowed the All-Father whole. Seconds later, however, Odin's son Vidar, god of vengeance, stabbed the monster in the heart, ending its life. As for the mighty Thor, he and his nemesis, Jormungander, finally came to death grips. When the serpent lunged at him, the red-bearded god swung his hammer, which smashed the attacker's brain to mush. But as the creature collapsed, some of its deadly venom splashed onto Thor, who fell to the ground, never to rise again.

The Twilight of the Gods

The gods did not chain Loki in the cave only to penalize him for his hand in Baldur's death. The Norns had predicted that the deity of deceit would help lead the forces of evil during Ragnarok. And Odin sought to neutralize the threat Loki might pose in the upcoming battle.

By this time, any hopes that the prophecy might be wrong had evaporated. To the gods' and humans' dismay, one after another, the events the Norns had claimed would occur shortly before the apocalypse actually took place. First, there arrived Fimbulvetr, a long, colder-than-normal winter in which crop failures occurred throughout the world and many people in Midgard starved to death. Next, three abnormally large roosters crowed so loudly that they could be heard worldwide. One of the birds warned the giants of the impending conflict. A second rooster alerted the humans. The third informed the Aesir. Among the latter, Heimdall now seized his trumpet and blasted a signal to the einherjar in Valhalla, telling those dead warriors that the day of the final fight had come.

As the echoes of those mighty horn blasts continued to reverberate across the realms, Odin stood at the forefront of a vast army of gods and human warriors and somberly marched them forward. In the distance, these fighters could see the multitudes of monsters and giants approaching to engage them in the great death struggle. So many marched on both sides that for hundreds of miles the ground shook, sending tremors through the trunk of the towering World Tree. In turn, the oceans churned and swirled, and mammoth waves pounded the beaches and flowed inland.

As the massive armies drew closer to each other, the forces of destruction that the Norns had long foreseen were unleashed. In his cavernous prison, Loki managed to break his bonds and rushed out to fight alongside his hideous offspring. One of those creatures, the giant wolf Fenrir, became so filled with rage that it shattered the supposedly unbreakable Gleipnir. Meanwhile, the serpentine monstrosity Jormungander pulled its miles-long bulk up onto the land, and Hel rose up from her murky realm hoping to take part in the impending fight.

Finally, the forces of good and evil came together in a colossal clash of unimaginable violence. One by one the gods, remaining valiant and noble to their last breaths, met their ends, as did the einherjar. The giants, dragons, Loki, and his nasty minions died too. Indeed, the titanic opposing forces proceeded to annihilate each other, causing the piles of the dead to steadily grow. Then, as if disheartened by the sheer horror of it all, the entire cosmos convulsed. "The earth shook, mountains crumbled," Mabie writes, and sheets of flame engulfed mighty Yggdrasil, which finally "fell into ashes." Eventually, all that was left was "a vast abyss filled with moaning seas and brooded over by a pale, colorless light."[36]

The Very Definition of Heroism

Long ages passed. It is unknown how many centuries elapsed after Ragnarok because no one was keeping track of such things anymore. It appeared that the wretched remains of the

This picture shows Ragnarok, a colossal battle between good and evil where the gods met their ends.

universe were lifeless and would remain so for eternity. But as it turned out, that was not to be. By some miracle—perhaps the result of small remnants of magic that had somehow survived in the ruins—floating pieces of the great tree began to clump together. In time they formed roots, which sent out shoots that would in due course grow into new realms.

Furthermore, all life had not been obliterated. The surviving wisps of magic had apparently kept two humans intact, preserving them in a deep sleep for countless centuries. A man named Lif and his wife, Lofthrasir, eventually awakened. To their surprise, they found that they had inherited a new cosmos that had been resurrected from the old one. And over the ensuing centuries, slowly but steadily, their offspring populated that new world.

Not all of the Norse believed in this optimistic myth of a magical aftermath to Ragnarok. A great many of them clung to the gloomier, more pessimistic tale that predicted the world would one day end permanently. But no matter which of those myths one accepted, all Vikings agreed on one point. Namely, their traditional gods had been supremely courageous figures to be admired and in some ways imitated. In fact, the Norse viewed the gods' ultimate sacrifice during Ragnarok as the very definition of heroism and honor and never ceased to be moved by it. In Daniel McCoy's words:

> How one met one's fate, whatever that fate happened to be, was what separated honorable and worthy people from the dishonorable and unworthy. Norse religion and mythology were thoroughly infused with this view. The gods . . . fought for themselves and their world tirelessly and unflinchingly, even though they knew that in the end that struggle was hopeless. . . . They went out not with a whimper, but a bang. This attitude is what made the Vikings the Vikings.[37]

Introduction: A World Filled with Wonder

1. Quoted in Kevin Crossley-Holland, *The Norse Myths*. New York: Pantheon, 1980, p. 148.
2. Daniel McCoy, *The Viking Spirit: An Introduction to Norse Mythology and Religion*. Self-published, CreateSpace Independent Publishing Platform, 2016, p. 59.
3. Daniel McCoy, "The Enchanted World," Norse Mythology for Smart People. https://norse-mythology.org.

Chapter One: The Era of Creation

4. Quoted in Daniel McCoy, trans., "Ginnungagap," Norse Mythology for Smart People. https://norse-mythology.org.
5. Crossley-Holland, *The Norse Myths*, p. xxxix.
6. Mircea Eliade, *Myth and Reality*. London: Allen and Unwin, 1964, p. 13.
7. Brian Branston, *Gods and Heroes from Viking Mythology*. New York: Peter Bedrick, 1994, p. 17.
8. Neil Gaiman, *Norse Mythology*. New York: Norton, 2017, pp. 32–33.
9. Branston, *Gods and Heroes from Viking Mythology*, p. 30.
10. Quoted in Gaiman, *Norse Mythology*, p. 71.
11. Quoted in Gaiman, *Norse Mythology*, pp. 71–72.
12. Branston, *Gods and Heroes from Viking Mythology*, p. 37.

Chapter Two: Realms of the Living

13. Quoted in Carolyne Larrington, trans., *The Poetic Edda*. New York: Oxford University Press, 2014, p. 66.
14. Quoted in Larrington, *The Poetic Edda*, pp. 66–67.
15. Quoted in Larrington, *The Poetic Edda*, p. 69.
16. Irina-Maria Manea, "The Contest Between Odin and Thor," World History Encyclopedia, March 2, 2021. www.worldhistory.org.
17. Quoted in Larrington, *The Poetic Edda*, p. 49.
18. Quoted in Larrington, *The Poetic Edda*, p. 50.

19. Daniel McCoy, "Thor's Hammer," Norse Mythology for Smart People. https://norse-mythology.org.
20. Quoted in Larrington, *The Poetic Edda*, p. 49.
21. Daniel McCoy, "Nidavellir/Svartalfheim," Norse Mythology for Smart People. https://norse-mythology.org.
22. McCoy, *The Viking Spirit*, pp. 148–49.
23. Donna Jo Napoli, *Treasury of Norse Mythology*. Washington, DC: National Geographic, 2015, p. 161.

Chapter Three: Realms of the Dead

24. Daniel McCoy, "Hel (The Underworld)," Norse Mythology for Smart People. https://norse-mythology.org.
25. Hamilton W. Mabie, *Norse Mythology: Great Stories from the Eddas*. Mineola, NY: Dover, 2015, pp. 72–73.
26. Quoted in Gaiman, *Norse Mythology*, p. 240.
27. Quoted in Noah Tetzner, "Valhalla: How Viking Belief in a Glorious Afterlife Empowered Warriors," History, March 3, 2021. www.history.com.
28. Crossley-Holland, *The Norse Myths*, p. xxx.
29. H.R.E. Davidson, *Gods and Myths of Northern Europe*. Baltimore, MD: Penguin, 1972, pp. 215–16.

Chapter Four: Apocalypse and Aftermath

30. Daniel McCoy, "Fate, Wyrd/Urd," Norse Mythology for Smart People. https://norse-mythology.org.
31. Edith Hamilton, *Mythology*. New York: Grand Central, 1999, p. 300.
32. McCoy, "Fate, Wyrd/Urd."
33. Branston, *Gods and Heroes from Viking Mythology*, p. 73.
34. Quoted in *The Prose Edda*, trans. Arthur G. Brodeur. New York: American-Scandinavian Foundation, 1916, p. 43.
35. Mabie, *Norse Mythology*, pp. 34–35.
36. Mabie, *Norse Mythology*, pp. 88–89.
37. McCoy, *The Viking Spirit*, pp. 289–90.

FOR FURTHER RESEARCH

Books

Padraic Colum, *Loki: The Mischief Behind the Legend*. Monument, CO: Wordfire, 2022.

Jason Dodd, *Norse Mythology: A Collection of the Best Norse Myths*. West Sacramento, CA: Rivercat, 2024.

Gunnar Hylnsson, *Norse Myths, Paganism, Magic, Vikings, and Runes*. Self-published, 2022.

Dorling Kindersley, *Eyewitness: Viking*. New York: Dorling Kindersley, 2024.

Mathias Nordwig, *Norse Mythology for Kids*. Eagle, ID: Rockridge, 2020.

Henry Romano, *Myths and Legends of the Norse*. London: DTTY, 2022.

Internet Sources

Thomas Apel, "Loki," Mythopedia, December 8, 2022. https://mythopedia.com.

Centre of Excellence, "Freya in Norse Mythology," February 24, 2024. www.centreofexcellence.com.

Historian's Hut, "The Myth of Nor and His Nor Way," July 26, 2019. https://thehistorianshut.com.

David Nikel, "Viking Religion: From the Norse Gods to Christianity," Life in Norway, August 21, 2019. www.lifeinnorway.net.

Rhianna Padman, "Norse Cosmology: What Does the Universe Look like in Norse Mythology?," The Collector, July 2, 2023. www.thecollector.com.

Jessica R. Scott, "Who Are the Jotnar in Norse Mythology?," Life in Norway, October 8, 2021. www.lifeinnorway.net.

Jessica Suess, "Fenrir: Who Was the Norse Wolf Destined to Kill Odin?," The Collector, April 26, 2024. www.thecollector.com.

Noah Tetzner, "Valhalla: How Viking Belief in a Glorious Afterlife Empowered Warriors," History, March 3, 2021. www.history.com.

Websites

Life in Norway

www.lifeinnorway.net/?s=mythology

This online guide to Norwegian life, culture, and history includes links to many articles about Norse mythology. The site includes articles about the World Tree, the gods and goddesses, and some of the many other creatures and beings found in Norse mythology.

Norse Mythology for Smart People

https://norse-mythology.org

Written by Daniel McCoy, a noted scholar of Norse myths and folklore, this site contains a rounded, detailed look at the Norse myths, with numerous links to supportive articles, including ones on the various Norse gods, Norse cosmology, Viking culture, and diverse Norse writings.

World History Encyclopedia

www.worldhistory.org

This free, online history resource has an extensive collection of articles on all aspects of Norse mythology. These articles can be found by typing "Norse mythology" or specific names (such as Odin) or events (such as Ragnarok) into the website search bar.

Note: Boldface page numbers indicate illustrations.

PICTURE CREDITS

Cover: Rawpixel.com/Shutterstock

8: Maury Aaseng
12: Sarunyu L/Shutterstock
14: Lebrecht Music & Arts/Alamy Stock Photo
17: Volgi archive/Alamy Stock Photo
23: Rawpixel.com/Shutterstock
25: Photo © Fine Art Images/Bridgeman Images
30: Chronicle/Alamy Stock Photo
34: Heritage Image Partnership Ltd/Alamy Stock Photo
36: Fototeca Gilardi/Bridgeman Images
41: Ivy Close Images/Alamy Stock Photo
45: British Library/Newscom
48: British Library/Newscom
52: Lebrecht Music & Arts/Alamy Stock Photo

ABOUT THE AUTHOR

Classical historian and award-winning author Don Nardo has written numerous acclaimed volumes about ancient civilizations and peoples. They include more than four dozen overviews of the mythologies of the Sumerians, Babylonians, Egyptians, Greeks, Romans, Persians, Celts, Chinese, Aztecs, Hindus, Native Americans, and others. Nardo, who also composes and arranges orchestral music, lives with his wife, Christine, in Massachusetts.